CHOICE REVIEW

SO-CKQ-968

DATE DUE

WITHDRAWN

A GYPSY'S HISTORY OF THE WORLD

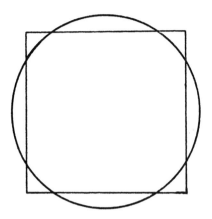

A GYPSY'S HISTORY OF THE WORLD

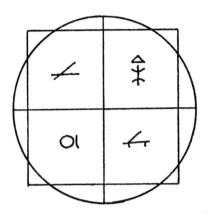

KIM ROBERT STAFFORD

Copper Canyon Press

1976

Some of these poems first appeared in: *Beloit Poetry Journal,*
Field, Loon, Luckiamute, Malahat Review, Mr. Cogito, Montana Gothic,
Northwest Review, Oregon Rainbow, Poetry Northwest, Portland Re-
view, Puerto Del Sol, Rapport, Small Farm, and *Wisconsin Review.*

811. S
S7785g
1976

Special thanks to Centrum Foundation, Fort Worden State
Park, where Copper Canyon is Press-in-Residence, and to
the National Endowment for the Arts, a federal agency,
for a grant which, in part, made this publication possible.

Thanks also to the National Endowment for
a Creative Writing Fellowship which allowed
the poet time to work at Copper Canyon
printing this book.

Copyright © 1976 by Kim Robert Stafford
Library of Congress Catalog Card: 76-39637
ISBN: 0-914742-25-6

Copper Canyon Press
Box 271
Port Townsend, WA 98368

SEQUENCE

THE TRAIL BEHIND

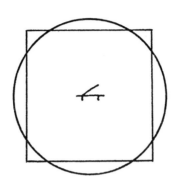

wind tugs leaves away
my hat begs to follow
guide me wind   the way
you're lost i'll be lost

DUETS

A dream flips me into the daylight.
I pry my way back:
a door opens, I enter, never
escape; the jailor sings by morning
duets through the bars with me.
I wake and out my window
by dawn a blackbird sings and
listens, sings and listens.

Listen. Thistledown jumps its dance
in the wind. I'm small and have
no regrets. Yesterday is a temporary
tombstone, a hollow stalk
on the hill. I'm putting my best
ear forward; in the space between songs
I'm travelling. My hands make
whistling wings in the wind.

No things meet without music:
wind and the chimney's whine, hail's click
with the pane, breath in a bird's
throat, rain in my ear when I
sleep in the grass. I miss the
whisper of a swallow's wings
meeting the thin air somewhere far.
Branches of my voice, come back.
Inside each song
I'm listening.

△

THE MOON

God's misspent dime climbs slowly
from its dark pocket in the hills.
An owl briefly knits song to silence,
the measured voice, the inner face
speaking breath to bone.

Inside, I am washing the dishes.
The power fails, lights flutter dark.
The plate I hold is all, single
link to the world, wet, smooth,
warm.
      I know it like the moon,
white, round mask of light
eclipsed, and now there is only this,
the plate, my hand, the clock, the owl,
and I caress it, as a blind man
the mirror.

SHAMAN

I hold my hand to the moon
and count the bones.
Then between my fingers each star
is a seed with no husk.
Between my palms is the last
grinding of wheat.

When everyone is asleep I trace
a number with flour on her cheek,
on his foot, and they are gone
by morning.

I go out into the new world,
hear their cries like leaves opening
from a stick. Weed stalks break;
seeds click from the pod; my
shirt like thistledown, I ask
the wind the way: Begin,
begin downwind. I tumble
to the water's edge.

On the river
yesterday's face slides past.
I kneel before the new ripple.

It has taken this long
for my hands
to fill with rain.

COVE

Milk covers the blue flowers
in the china bowl. She lived
alone north of Three-rocks
at the coast. Wind moved
past the chimney: Ave, Ave.

The flowers embroidered on
grandma's night-gown are nearly
worn away. The buttons sewn
with strands of grey hair
are polished like real pearls.
Her name is stitched at the hem
in blue: Eva.

I find this at the Good-will.

PROPOSAL

The sign for our town
has fallen off the road
into the field.
Wheat gives with the wind.

Bending, the stalks drop seed.
The bearded ears of winter
wheat have their own
whispered song. May our
town's defeat be graceful.

Past where the edge of town was,
sit in the wheat and ask
a friend her name. Rain
is coming; don't get up.

YARROW

rain walks across my back
as I bend to pick yarrow
herb forgotten by the road
waiting for a tired man
who knows the secret

three green leaves between two fingers
crushed   the breath of earth
held before the face   the bowl
of hands surround the taking in
of spirit   yarrow whispers

rain drips from my hatbrim
each hand wears a glove of scent
the road reflects the sky   each
blackbird in the willow hedge
sings praise of yarrow

who knows the secret   a man
waiting by the road   a stalk
of yarrow bending for the rain
I walk across the sky's reflection
convinced by yarrow

)))

RESIDENCE IN GRIZZLY

They still own one patch of stony ground,
an island of weeds in the miles of wheat.
The last, mute shepherd from the hills,
might come to the porch at Christmas,
his flute taken for a coyote's howl
emerging from the wind.

In winter walking home we listen to each
coyote; surrounding the field of stones
the fence of rust wire hums
like the song we learned
from the people we drove away.

01

HISTORIC MARKER

it was here in mid-winter
they paused to ask each
other the way   the trail
behind filling with snow

> *that broken tree   avalanche*
> *kill   do you remember*
> *late summer   we saw*
> *the break up twenty feet*
> *now here at eye level   deep*
> *snow   bring that day back*
> *speak   are we here*

it was here they built a fire
warmed their hands and faces
until the embers sank
hissed deep in the tunnel
of smoke   here they turned
to look back with the wind
find their tracks nearly gone
then set out uphill   the people
crossing the mountains to find
bitterroot hidden one wealthy day
in a cave on the other side

and here where the wind
slowed just below the summit
they paused to tap out a
song with stiff knuckles
at the base of the last cliff

       we are here   hungry children
       mountain forget   we will remember
       wind forget   fill our trail
       we will remember   avalanche
       be patient   we will disappear
       without your help

it is here   driver   the signs
plastered with snow forget
their names   but you know
the road is endless either way
your car in its brief life
will never fail   the radio
sings what your money can buy

but driver   recall how here
they paused   teeth chattering
a brief prayer   near where
you kneel in the snow
to put on your chains

4

ORCAS ISLAND

*It is surrounded by water
because it is an island.*
                    — *Exile*

Blackbird dead on the road
raised one wing for the wind
I was walking
                    with a scar
on my strongest arm
I came here myself

When wind blows sand   blink
heron with its feet in the ditch
jumps up   flies off
                    the horizon
makes me alone
heart is the only voice
this is one way to keep from being cold

Find a dark place and close your mouth
there is a roof here
I come in where the door hung
once   brambles come in
at a crack in the wall
I take off my hat

Snow has nowhere else to go
falls here   wind brings it in
I scrape straw for cover
in a corner

In cold weather be cold

GABERLUNZIE

No-one knows where their name came from,
those beggars with bags full of holes
and chains of keys, going sane and crazy
with the moon's changes, pleading money
and throwing it away.

If we listen fiercely enough, they tell truth.
Spreading the cards for those poor in
fortune, they hum the trance of five
left hands, thumbs to little fingers linked.
The quintet of right hands are wild
in rings of silver and stone.

On the road their cats are gibbering
lunatics, chasing mice down the long rut
from here to the end. The men, old as owls,
at dusk beg a bushel of wheat and locusts,
strike fire by the river to feast. Lucky
dogs loose in the world, they mutter
their creed like frogs and fill their shoes
with grass.

☉

BUM

Following his crooked track I
found him under the bridge,
shared a bottle of red,
cottonwood fire.
                    Five red lines
made a lady on the wall;
hunters in blue chalk
crouched for the kill.
My friend, knowing the artist, said:
"He never could tell a woman
from lipstick."

+

SPANISH MUSEUM

They were different then, said our guide.
Artists thought they had to be crazy.
Perception possessed them.
This man, he was dying
as he painted this same nude again
and again. She became a nun
when he died. Look at her eyes.
She knew the light of her body
was making him blind.

☦

VIGILANCE

wherever I look birds land
hemlock tip bent east   pine bough
rooftop where crow renounces
all claim to grace   keeps watch
in the empty place no-one else
would take

if I rise why shouldn't the roses
and if the buds around me open
will I find my tiniest leaf
tucked from the inside out
into the world

wind throws birds across the sky
thorns hold my coat together
if I do not move
someone far away is calling
if I answer I may never
hear them again

A HAND'S MUSIC

I'm hiding in my hands
the most exquisite scar
the left palm   spiral
web of cuts   the stroke
of corrugated tin as I
fell
       I show the center
of a rose when the
fingers unfold   such
deep design and perfect
form   as when the hive
is winter-killed   we peel
the comb apart to find
each cell holding a bee
the still cluster of workers
packed at the center
like seed in a sunflower

I wrap this gift again
inside my hand
I a survivor listening
to the scar's tiny pulse
such an offering
as the dead bees hum

INSIDE THE FENCE:
Tule Lake Internment Camp

The violinist tamed the birds,
fastened branches to the wall,
offered crumbs between his whistling lips.
The children, when it didn't rain,
had to fill a hole with water
so they could see the sky ringed
by earth, their faces wind wrinkled.

Walking was the favorite sport,
finding things, bringing them back
to talk about over tea.
                          We live
this way still, though they say
the war is ended, we can go away.
They took the fences down.
                          Walking
is still the favorite sport, offering
a shoulder to any bird, watching the sky
in a puddle. Our faces wrinkle
for the old days, when we were confined.

△

THE BASKET DEEP

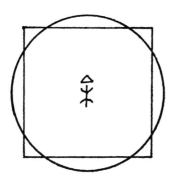

VILLANELLE FOR THE SPIDERS

The smallest weavers work at night
To link together all they know
And build their web that holds our light.

It's drops of dew that catch my sight
And tell me, when through dawn I go,
That smallest weavers work at night.

I find the spiral fabric slight
And wonder how they spin so slow
Yet build their web that holds our light.

A touch could tear, my deep breath might
Destroy the net their trust put low,
For smallest weavers work at night.

Patience is life and their delight,
Ready again if wind should blow
To build their web that holds our light.

Our feeble threads are strung so tight
Across the darkness deep below.
The smallest weavers work at night
To build their web that holds our light.

A GYPSY'S HISTORY
OF THE WORLD

before sunrise hides all stars
reach to learn by braille
the single turning constellation
dewfall in the grass

> *four-cornered circle spins*
> *without a sound*
> *four-cornered circle*
> *not one made by hand*

in sleep a silent bird has
deepest song   a tree's heart still
a flower's rainbow root-held
not to be

> *four-cornered circle seems*
> *right perfect round*
> *four-cornered circle*
> *not one made by hand*

who owns this restless earth
the nation of the dead and yet
unborn   we who walk here now
take care

> *four-cornered circle turns*
> *all over this dark ground*
> *four-cornered circle*
> *not one made by hand*

step into the spreading shadow
the cave in what we know
colors are less than the crow
who wears them

    four-cornered circle grows
    in the island mound
    four-cornered circle
    not one made by hand

a leaf remembers its form
seed after seed   with every
constellation of fingertips
a hand recalls the world

    four-cornered circle spins
    without a sound
    four-cornered circle
    not one made by hand

IN SEARCH OF BIRDS

In the world-mirror bluebirds see a tree,
And flying there, take me with their song;
Then it's the click of beak to glass I hear—
Reflection-met, the birds now on the ground.
Then I wake and feel my broken wing
Within the dream that somehow numbed my hand.

Sawing wood I halt the swing of hand
And walk to where a dead and empty tree
Is black with starlings, each lost leaf a wing
That flutters in the wind. Their single song
Is steady until dusk: across the open ground
We feel the owl's hunger, then we hear.

At noon the blackbird's warning-call I hear.
As I cut willow stems my careless hand
Has nearly touched the nest: above the ground
But inches, woven grass, moss from a tree,
Someone's hair. Beneath that frightened song
The young are folded featherless wing on wing.

I find a feather, then a little wing,
Then many tiny bones, This time I hear
Only the wind in pines around, the song
That led me out. I climb until my hand
Has found the single smooth branch, the tree
Swaying this hawk's-perch far above the ground.

Lamenting, a killdeer limps across the ground,
Pretending for my sake a broken wing.
Here in the open far from any tree
I seek the nest like stones in sand, then hear
Above my head the father bird. My hand
Pulls low the hat that guards me from that song.

More like an insect chirp or buzz their song,
Nighthawks high and racing for the ground—
There they flutter like a twitch of hand,
A sudden thunder in their flight, each wing
Resounding against the wind. It's then I hear
The world-duet that branches like a tree.

Leaf by leaf the tree responds to song
That generations hear within the ground
Where any wing or leaf could be your hand.

FORSYTH LIBRARY
FORT HAYS STATE

MARRIAGE

Wind-devils spin dust on the slope of sage;
a pale billboard staggers in the gulley:
"Graves Hotel—Deep Sleep Guaranteed."
Over the tall, long hills of Montana
we are driving east for a wedding
farther away than we've ever been.
> *dream alone—*
> *sleep all night*
> *then wake the light of day.*

I swerve around a pair of doves
searching the pavement for the perfect
speck of gravel, that bit of earth
that keeps you alive. Blackbird's beak
is a split seed, its song a root all the great
plains deep, our trip a long listening.
> *red-wing sing—*
> *for all i've lost,*
> *for all i've tossed away.*

At the river I gather water in my hat.
It's early yet and Dolly Varden rise,
those supple fish named for the girl who
danced so well in dim light long ago.
I water the steaming engine. Each butterfly
on the radiator grill is courted by a yellowjacket.
> *dolly varden dance*
> *but give your answer soon—*
> *else i'll take that honeymoon alone.*

I think it's someone hitch-hiking, an old man,
trunk bleached white, bark in shreds
hanging to the ground, a single, twisted
limb beckoning. The white line flicks away
like heartbeats racing into the past toward home.

> *thin white hand—*
> *where have you been*
> *now you there in the wind.*

A constellation of white crosses sway
where the guard rail is gone,
a five-cross curve, a family
carried off like sparrows billowing,
the wind's strange custom of remembering,
to touch and move all creatures
in a single turn.

> *at graves hotel—*
> *i'll meet you there*
> *and we will marry then.*

HALFWAY HOME

1.

I am walking home.
Halfway up the street I stare
into a hole in the yard, opened where a
fir tree fell: a ten-dollar bill lies there.
I knock on the door; the woman and her
oldest daughter, both gray, invite me in.
I sit in the largest chair.
"Leave the money there," she says,
"Ransom for my husband, dead so young—
it's for the wind."
Outside I look at the ten again:
one side is blank, the other counterfeit.

2.

My brother and I have climbed the highest
hill to lean against the wind.
A round stone rolls from underfoot
to bound down the long green slope.
It's wrong and lovely when we bend
to pry another boulder from the turf,
let it go and feel its fading
heartbeat in our feet.
Then we stare into the hole it left:
a diary pressed there against the earth
so long it's green, and our four hands
are gentle as the words are dim,
until the wind explodes its pages
to the sky, and we are running,
always running.

3.

Surviving still, I learn that
to be born is to be halfway home.
And these words now, my nearest
counterfeit for truth, are ransom
for the dead, one careful gesture
no matter how weak, delivered
to the wind.

ɯ

IN THE NEEDLE'S EYE

No matter how fast a river flows,
it's not alive; no matter how
slow a cricket creeps, it is.
And all over the sycamore the buds
are slowly taking off their bandages,
asking of the world only another leaf,
another leaf, until the whole tree
happens, the opening movement easy
because it will close and wither.

It's like chalk on the sidewalk,
a child's old geography, sequence of
small feet skipping past the box
where the stone fell, the dance
and song toward the last number
distant, always visible.

2.

No matter how green new leaves turn,
they're not forever; no matter how
dark the night sky dreams, it is.
And the bone needle threaded
with breath stitches one day tight
to the next, the seam a spiral clasped,
sun-button sewn, moon-pendant
suspended by a thread until
the needle's eye is suddenly opened
when the worn strand snaps.

It's like standing in the field of dew,
closing your hands around a clod
to concentrate what you have learned
from gravity, to strike the seed's
green spark.

3.

No matter how long the lamp burns
it flickers blind; no matter how
brief the cricket's song, it sings.
And always about genesis a stillness,
a waiting for light, for water, the word,
a necklace of seeds strung on a silver
wire, a needle that plows dark earth
under the small voice:

> *i am my own seed still,*
> *for the seed survives*
> *in its being, and after*
> *if rain prevail.*

THE BASKET DEEP

The wild honey man is walking on our street.
He listens at the flower places, bramble
trellises, cherry trees broken into bloom
to find the bees and follow them home.

From the basket wide and deep,
My Lord,
All seed is cast aside.

The wild honey man never wears a hat
and sings, his hair thin, coat
patched with holes, yet he's never
stung. He has the quiet eyes.

In the summer warm and green,
My Lord,
The pollen all will swarm.

We followed him once when he
followed the bees. Head in the sky
on the humming nectar path, he'd pause
and listen for the next bee's coming.

In the standing field so tall,
My Lord,
By the scythe brought low at last.

He chased us back that day,
fire in one hand, ax in the other.
His whiskers in the sun glistened
with the last honeycomb he'd chewed.

> *On the threshing floor alone,*
> *My Lord,*
> *Beneath thy flail so long.*

We saw him in the afternoon emerging
from the woods with a pail, brushing
numbed bees out of his hair
so they stuck to his hand.

> *In the winnow wind so high,*
> *My Lord,*
> *All seed that falls is thine.*

The wild honey man is walking on our street,
hive-sweet, tree-handsome. She buys,
standing in her garden humming, tries to offer
him an iris, but cannot break the stem.

> *In the basket wide and deep,*
> *My Lord,*
> *In the basket wide and deep.*

EARLY RISER

The home-map glimmers in a swallow's eye,
eager mirror hunting the north star.
Circling constellations stare, an ancestor
flock re-living each night the long circuit,
an old one plunging in a blaze of feathers.

In the rush of its own wind the flyway dips
toward earth, dawn star's declination beckoning.
A globe of dew shows the whole sky
when the beak sips it. With a leaf
for shade each fist of feathers must rest
to rise at dusk, the map of this dark world
in its eye.

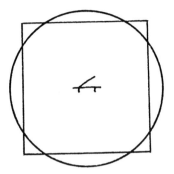

GYPSY ROAD SIGNS

⧸	*one travels*
△	*here one can speak truth*
△\	*be on guard*
⚹	*one is confined*
╪	*one is driven away*
+	*here is nothing to be found*
�111	*we have already stolen*
⚹	*here one loved a woman*
≋	*here one wished himself children*
⟊	*wedding in sight*
⊙	*generous & true men*
∮	*good people*
O\	*we have hidden ourselves*
⤙	*we will come again*

Translated by the poet from the German of
Wolf in der Maur, *Die Zigeuner*, Wien: 1969,
pp. 183-184.

100 copies printed letterpress from hand set 14 pt. Centaur type on Rives buff lightweight paper by the poet, and bound in cloth over boards by Lincoln & Allen, Portland.

1500 copies photo-offset from the letterpress original.